332.6028
B645t

BST

THE TRILLIONAIRE NEXT DOOR

THE
TRILLIONAIRE
NEXT
DOOR

THE GREEDY INVESTOR'S GUIDE TO DAY TRADING

Andy Borowitz

HarperBusiness
An Imprint of HarperCollins*Publishers*

332. 6028 B645t

THE TRILLIONAIRE NEXT DOOR. Copyright © 2000 by Andy Borowitz. All rights reserved. Printed in the United States of America. No part of this book may be used or reproduced in any manner whatsoever without written permission except in the case of brief quotations embodied in critical articles and reviews. For information address HarperCollins Publishers Inc., 10 East 53rd Street, New York, NY 10022.

HarperCollins books may be purchased for educational, business, or sales promotional use. For information please write: Special Markets Department, HarperCollins Publishers Inc., 10 East 53rd Street, New York, NY 10022.

FIRST EDITION

Designed by Elliott Beard

Printed on acid-free paper

Library of Congress Cataloging-in-Publication Data has been applied for.

ISBN 0-06-662076-7

00 01 02 03 04 ❖/RRD 10 9 8 7 6 5 4 3 2 1

FEB 27 '0

THIS BOOK IS DEDICATED TO OPRAH WINFREY.

*Whether or not it is chosen to be a selection of Oprah's Book Club
and goes on to sell millions of copies, thank you, Oprah,
for being the wonderful and inspiring person that you are.*

I love you with all my might.

CONTENTS

Who Wants to Be a Millionaire . . . When You Could Be a Trillionaire Instead?

I kept hearing about complete idiots who were
getting rich off the Internet—and I thought,
Why not me?

—Becky Holcomb, day trader

If you want to become a millionaire by trading stocks on the Internet, you've picked up the wrong book.

If, however, you want to become a *trillionaire*—and learn how I did it—read on.

It may seem as though I'm splitting hairs. You're probably saying, "Millionaire, trillionaire, what's the difference—rich is rich, right?"

Wrong.

The Myth of the Millionaire

Right now, we live in a culture obsessed with millionaires. People buy lottery tickets, go on game shows, and even marry Donald Trump, all in the hopes of becoming one. And I think that it's sad—sad that they're setting their sights *so low.*

Please don't misunderstand me. I don't have anything against millionaires—I hire them all the time. Millionaires have very pleasant lifestyles: expensive cars, fancy houses, and the best plastic surgery and antidepressants that money can buy. But one nagging fact remains: There's nothing *special* about being a millionaire.

Why? Quite simply, there are just too many ways to become one. You could record a hit CD, star in a movie, play center on an NBA team, or invent something like the VCR or the automobile—and just like that, you're a millionaire.

And those aren't the only ways. You could be hurled from a roller coaster, slam your head against the pavement, and sue the theme park. That's a million dollars right there. Then, when the surgeon who operates on your brain screws up and leaves a sponge in your head, you could sue him. That's another cool mill. On the way home from the hospital, the ambulance driver jumps the curb and smashes into a brick wall . . . would a call to your lawyer be in order? By now I think you probably agree with me: It's just too easy to become a millionaire.

As a result, we have more millionaires in this country than at any other time in our history. I don't have any hard statistics on this, but I'm willing to bet that one out of four Americans is a millionaire. At the very least, it's one out of five.

Still think millionaires are special? Still eager to join the burgeoning, unruly herd of dime-a-dozen, anyone-can-be-one millionaires? Or is there something inside you, something in the back of your head, a little voice that's saying, "I'm better than that!"

I'm sure some people will say it's greedy to want to be a trillionaire. They'll say, "Okay, so maybe millionaires are no big deal nowadays, but there's nothing wrong with being, say, a *billionaire*."

That's true. There's nothing wrong with being a billionaire.

Or is there?

The Myth of the Billionaire

Let's take one of our most famous billionaires, Bill Gates, founder and "chief software architect" of Microsoft. He's built the largest corporation in America, and his software products are the most widely used in the world. He's accomplished an impressive amount, especially for a geek with a speaking voice straight out of *Sesame Street.*

When all is said and done, who wouldn't want to be Bill Gates?

Me, that's who.

Gates's fortune is nothing to sneeze at, but let's not kid ourselves—he's still working for "The Man." He has to face off with angry stockholders and testify to Congress, and, worst of all, he has to wear a suit and tie while he's doing it. He might dream of being his own boss someday, but he never will be. He's like a mouse running on a wheel, chasing billion-dollar bonuses instead of cheese—and going nowhere fast.

Can Bill Gates work at home, the way I do? Can he stay in his bathrobe for three days in a row, shaving and showering only as he pleases? Can he just drop everything and turn off his computer when there's a really awesome *Buffy* rerun on?

Let's keep in mind, too, the devastating "opportunity cost" Gates is paying, stuck in a dead-end job that will never, and I mean *never,* make him a trillionaire. I hate to rub it in, but while that all-day sucker known as Bill Gates is wasting the best years of his life at Microsoft, I'm buying *and* selling Microsoft—often in the space of three minutes! So, you tell me: Who's working for whom—and who's the *real* boss?

And what about another billionaire, Ted Turner? When the AOL-Time Warner merger was announced, Turner's stake in the company was valued at $9 billion. Impressive?

We day traders have a term for $9 billion: "chump change."

I'm sure by now you've come to the same conclusion I arrived at long, long ago: Being a billionaire is better than being a million-aire—*but not by much.*

Am I being greedy? Perhaps. But "greedy is better than needy." Don't take my word for it—I've got a pillow with that exact saying on it. And pillows don't lie.

So, now that we agree that both millionaires and billionaires suck, let's get down to brass tacks: Being a trillionaire is the only game in town. And there's only one way to become one.

The Only Way to Become One

You can only become a trillionaire by day trading.

If you choose this new career, you won't be alone. Five years ago, no one traded stocks online, but today over one-quarter of all investors are trading electronically. Do the math: At this rate, in twenty years, there will be more day traders in the United States than people.

If you're new to the world of day trading, though, it's only fair to point out that you're a little late to the party. This wild, frothing bull market has been raging for years now. While you sat there twiddling your thumbs, your friends, relatives, and neighbors all grew egre-giously rich, buying wide-screen TVs the size of barns and SUVs powerful enough to splatter a moose.

Having missed the boat up until now, it's understandable that you're impatient, anxious, and more than a little desperate—you'll do *anything* to get started day trading.

This book is for desperate people like you—when getting rich quick just isn't fast enough.

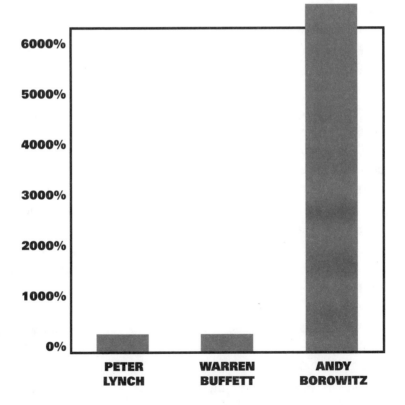

A Trillion with Your Name on It

Remember this basic economic fact: There is a limited, finite number of dollars in the world. They're not printing any more of them. So don't let some other clown walk off with the trillion that are rightfully yours. You've worked long and hard reading this chapter—you *deserve* to be a trillionaire, and you shouldn't let anyone or anything stand in your way!

You're excited now, I'm sure. Your heart is racing, and beads of sweat are appearing on your forehead. Perhaps, and this is just a guess, you even need to go to the bathroom. That's what the rush of day trading feels like, multiplied by ten—or maybe twenty if you have a really fast modem.

I know—you're ready to grab a mouse and start pointing and clicking. You're ready to make that first trade, the trade that, all day traders say, you never forget for the rest of your life. But before we go any further, it's time for a gut check.

Do you have what it takes to be a day trader?

Like the video game "Tomb Raider," day trading is not for the faint of heart. Unlike "Tomb Raider," there are just a lot of numbers on the screen and no hot babes in leather thongs. Like "Tomb Raider," though, once you start day trading it is hard to stop, even when your mom is yelling at you to get dressed and go get a "real" job.

Like G-force to a jet pilot, the power of day trading can blow you away, stretching and pulling your face into myriad weird shapes. So before we begin, ask yourself these questions:

- Are you man enough? Or, if you're a woman, are you person enough?

- Do you think the sky's the limit—when all of the so-called experts are saying it's falling?

- Do you think the glass is half empty or half full—or, like me, do you just go ahead and buy the glass?

- And do you have the guts to sell that same glass five minutes later?

I hope that the answer to these questions is yes. I hope you have the courage, boldness, and vision to join me in this great adventure, on the front lines of an economic revolution that will make the way stocks used to be traded seem as obsolete as a month-old cell phone.

Strap yourself in, Day Trader. And hang on for the wildest ride of your life.

Let's go!

Who I Am and How I Did It

Everybody goes into day trading for different
reasons, but in my case, it was getting kicked
out of law school that really got me started.

—Ned Leavitt, day trader

On the wall over my computer, next to my poster of Sable, there hangs a plaque with this saying on it: "Only a fool would follow stock-market advice without knowing its source." I'm not sure who said that, but I couldn't agree more.

For this reason, I wouldn't expect you to follow any of the advice I dispense in this book without first knowing more about me: who I am and how I did it, my hopes, my dreams, my sorrows, and my triumphs.

How did I get to be a day-trading trillionaire? Am I smarter than you? No. Am I luckier than you? No. Am I sexier than you? Yes. But sexiness has nothing to do with it—because I only became sexy, truly sexy, *after* I became a trillionaire.

The fact is, I'm *exactly like you,* only richer.

Who I Am

I wasn't always pulling down a salary in the high thirteen figures. Far from it. Two years ago, I was working at a fast-food restaurant, which, for the purposes of this story, will remain nameless.

I had a job in the kitchen, assembling Whoppers. As pleasant as the work was, I sensed that my chances for advancement were poor. There's a "dirty little secret" about fast-food restaurants—they're hotbeds of favoritism and cutthroat politics. In the case of this particular franchise, there was a "glass ceiling" in effect for anyone who wasn't on the good side of the restaurant's manager, one James "Jimmy" Mandeville.

What did it take to get on his bad side? Practically any little thing. Anything from showing up for work two hours late to accidentally starting a grease fire that burns down half of the restaurant and forces it to close down for six weeks while the insurance investigators try to determine whether it was done on purpose or not. At any rate, I sensed that my future lay elsewhere.

There is a moment in every day trader's life, a moment of awakening, if you will, when he knows that day trading is the destiny that fate has chosen for him. My moment of awakening came one afternoon as I was putting together a Whopper With Cheese. It was a special order—hold the pickle, hold the lettuce. And as I held the pickle, I came to a sudden realization: The customer was having it *his* way. And I wanted to have it *my* way.

At that moment, I knew that my days at that unnamed restaurant were over. I ate the half-assembled Whopper, walked out of the restaurant, and never looked back. I wasn't going to spend the rest of my life "holding the pickle."

I realized that if I could be my own boss, the only ass I would ever have to kiss would be *my* ass.

How I Did It

I had heard about day trading before, from a coworker who had done so well at it that he was able to cut back his hours at the fry-machine from ten to a scant eight. Naturally, I had been intrigued by the concept of any venture that could provide someone with this level of freedom and independence.

Once I had my heart set on this new career, I immersed myself in day trading with a level of intensity and concentration I used to reserve for watching *The X-Files.*

I voraciously devoured every commercial about online trading I saw on TV. I studied the works of all of the world's most noted economists—not just Bill Griffeth and David Faber, but Ron Insana, Sue Herera, and Joe Kernen. I watched *Wall Street Week with Louis Rukeyser,* enduring horrible, witless puns for the sake of my quest. I bought a new mouse. I bought a Big Gulp. I got into my pajamas and stayed there.

I didn't become a day trader lickety-split. It took hard work and long, tedious hours of studying, with only the briefest of breaks— usually to stick a Hot Pocket in the microwave.

At the end of this arduous process, I was able to distill all I had learned into a set of rules I came to call "The Ten Principles of Day Trading." These scientifically tested principles became the foundation for my infomercials, my edu-tational tape series, and the book you now hold in your hands.

By reading this book, you will learn in a mere thirty minutes what took me over two weeks to learn.

What else is there to know about me? I'll refer you now to the FAQs (Frequently Asked Questions) that have received the most hits on my website, www.sexytrillionaire.com:

If you're a trillionaire, why do you need to sell books and tapes?

I want you to know, right off the bat, that I resent both the premise and the tone of that question. I'm going to have to ask you to rephrase it.

Sorry. Why did you write this book?

By writing this book—as well as by selling my tapes and my full line of Trillionaire accessories and intimate attire—I'm sharing the wealth that I've been fortunate enough to make through the miracle of day trading. Call me old-fashioned, but I firmly believe that it is the obligation of any trillionaire to reach out and be charitable to those less fortunate than he, even when they seem like real losers.

Why do you still live at home with your parents in their condo in San Diego?

Believe me, I've been trying to move into the twenty-four-room French Normandy–style mansion I recently bought in the affluent community of Palos Verdes, California. But I'm so busy trading my multi-trillion-dollar account, when do I have the time?

Actually, living with my parents is fine. They don't like my tying up the phone line as much as I do, and they do drop subtle "hints" from time to time about my moving out. And they don't make it a big secret that they wish I had gone to business school, the way their friends Bob and Dottie Halpern's precious son Josh did. But all in all, it's a good arrangement.

I just wish they understood a little bit better what I do for a living.

Getting Started

Day trading is like a swimming pool with no
water in it—you just have to dive right in.

—Buck Cantrell, day trader

I have one piece of sound advice for anyone contemplating an exciting career in day trading: Before you get started, quit your day job.

That's right, blow it off—not tomorrow, and not the day after tomorrow. Quit your day job *today.*

This is a vitally important first step. Day trading is a full-time job, and any "real" job you have will only prove to be a distraction. Therefore, it is imperative that you divest yourself of all other gainful employment, pronto.

I'll go one step further: When you quit your day job, don't do it in an amicable way that will leave the door even slightly ajar for your eventual return. Instead, create an ugly scene that will make your departure as painful and permanent as a thigh tattoo.

Why is this necessary? If, in the back of his mind, the day trader thinks he has an escape route—something to fall back on—it will take his "eyes off the prize," as it were, and adversely affect his investment results.

How to Quit

How should you quit? There are as many ways of quitting as there are quitters, but here are four surefire ways to quit your day job in a messy, irrevocable manner:

- Tell your boss that he's a cretin.

- Tell your boss that his wife is (a) ugly or (b) "a ho."

- Punch your boss in the face.

- Punch your boss's wife in the face.

If quitting isn't your thing, get yourself fired. Downloading company secrets onto your laptop will usually do the trick. Sending "inappropriate" jokes on the company's E-mail system is a surefire way, too. If neither of those work, I recommend that you sexually harass somebody. That's sure to get you bounced—and you can usually do it without even trying to.

The Ten Principles of Day Trading: How I Made Them Up

Once you get the basics down, it's incredible
how much you don't have to know.

—John Lescher, day trader

Ever since I became a full-time day trader, I have been called
everything from "a cyber-speculator" to "an embarrassment to your
father and me." Contrary to what its critics may think, however, day
trading is a science, like chemistry or astrology, with its own rigor-
ously tested set of principles.

When I first started touring the country, speaking to groups both
large and small about "The Ten Principles of Day Trading," people
looked at me as though I was out of my mind, on hemp, or both.
Some even called the police. And so I stopped touring the country,

had my name legally changed, and recorded a series of edu-tational cassettes.

Somehow, what had sounded insane as I shouted and flailed my arms in the Renaissance Room of the Gainesville ThriftySuites Hotel sounded perfectly reasonable as it played on my customers' car stereos—particularly when they were driving home from a bad job interview.

Suddenly, my revolutionary ideas about day trading were gaining traction. A wildfire was spreading across the country, and it was a pretty heady feeling to know that I was the guy with the matches and the gasoline. As one of my first customers wrote to me, back in those early, exciting days, "Look, I've tried everything else—I might as well try this."

Rules, Tools, and Fools

What are "The Ten Principles of Day Trading"? Simply put, they are the rock-solid, scientific rules you need to know before you begin. You wouldn't perform open-heart surgery without first going through four years of medical school; similarly, you shouldn't risk your life savings on the Internet without spending the thirty minutes it takes to learn these rules.

One caveat, however, right at the outset. "The Ten Principles of Day Trading" are so densely packed with information that it is inadvisable to read them straight through. You may find that they make your head throb with pain. You might experience dizziness or nausea and might require immediate hospitalization.

To put it another way, if "The Ten Principles of Day Trading" could be converted to pill form, the resulting pill would be big enough to choke a horse.

Therefore, for safety reasons, I have included several short rest-chapters I call "First Person"—first-person accounts of real, live day traders whose stories are an inspiration to us all. Meet these dedicated men and women, warts and all—literally, in some cases. Enter the anything-goes, roller-coaster world of these economic revolutionaries where Mountain Dew is drunk by the gallon, snoozing means losing, and showers are for wimps.

A Guarantee That's Hard to Believe

I believe so completely in my day trading system that I'm willing to make the following ironclad guarantee:

If you follow "The Ten Principles of Day Trading" to the letter, I guarantee that you will increase the volatility of your portfolio by 2,000 percent.

That's right, I said 2,000 percent.

If for some reason you fail to achieve these results, mail me a check in the amount you paid for this book, and I will send you a brand-new copy of the book, *free of charge.*

HOW DAY TRADING WORKS

BUY STOCK → VISIT SEX SITES → SELL STOCK → BECOME TRILLIONAIRE

Know the Lingo

As far as the jargon of economics goes,
I've found that if a word's not in your
computer's spell-check dictionary,
it's probably not worth knowing.

—Hal Shipley, day trader

Like any science, day trading has its own peculiar and arcane lexicon that must be learned before you make that first, sweet trade. Many budding day traders give me a blank stare when I tell them this—often, I discover, because they don't know what the words "arcane" and "lexicon" mean.

Let's put it another way—you wouldn't become a mechanic without knowing the meaning of technical terms like "carburetor" and "wheel." Similarly, no beginning day trader should start throwing around phrases like "I've been riding the mo all day" without fully comprehending what he has just said.

As important as knowing the terminology may be, I'm saddened and surprised by the number of would-be day traders who never get started because, quite simply, they think they will never master this specialized lingo. Let me share with you a letter I received (via "snail-mail"—a *very* bad sign!) from an aspiring day trader who had purchased my series of edu-tational cassettes:

Dear Mr. Sexy Trillionaire,

    I'm very interested in learning how to day trade, but I'm really intimidated by all of the words you have to know. When I see economists and stock-market experts on TV, sometimes I have a really hard time understanding what they're talking about. "Limit order," "high beta," "Fibonacci amplification"—it seems as though the stock market is a lot more complicated than you make it sound on your three-minute tapes.

    I've been wondering whether or not I should go to business school to learn what economics are all about before I start risking a lot of my money in the market. What do you think—is business school a good investment?

Signed,
Confused

When I first read this letter, I felt nothing but sympathy for its author. You're bound to go through life feeling somewhat perplexed and addled when you've been born with a name like "Confused." What were his parents thinking?

It's Geek to Me

True, when you see economists on TV, the jargon they use is often dense and confusing. But there's a simple reason for that—*they want it to be that way.*

    You see, the Wall Street professionals want you to be intimidated, to keep you on the sidelines. They don't want you to take part in this economic miracle. They want to keep the Rolls Royces, the Bose Wave radios, and the expensive second wives all to themselves. When they throw around tricky terms that you don't understand, like "volume" and "yield," remember: It's just another case of "The Man" trying to keep you down!

And they would just love to see easily snookered wimps like "Confused" "out of the mix" and enrolled in business school for two years—while they busily scoop up all the Qualcomm stock until there's no more to go around!

This, I'm afraid, is an example of one of the sad facts about the business world that we will encounter many times in the course of this book: Economists are sneaky douchebags.

The Key to Understanding Tricky Things That Are Hard to Understand

The "dirty little secret" about the terminology of economics is this: Anyone can understand it, if you just use a little common sense.

Let's take the term "large cap." We hear a lot nowadays about large-cap companies, large-cap stocks, large-cap funds, large-cap this, large-cap that. What exactly are people talking about?

Let's take McDonald's, one of the best known of the large-cap companies, as an example. What makes it one? If you walk into any of its restaurants, you will notice—if you look closely enough—that *all of the employees are wearing large caps.*

Now that wasn't so hard, was it?

Just as a child learning to read is told to "sound it out" when he encounters a word he doesn't know, I exhort you to "think it through" when you come across some obscure financial jargon you don't understand. Nine times out of ten, you'll be right.

Here's an example of thinking it through. At one of my day trading seminars held on a riverboat in Mississippi, an audience member asked me a question using a term with which I was unfamiliar. This was how our exchange went:

AUDIENCE MEMBER: Would you ever consider trading futures?
ME: No, thank you—I have no idea what your future is, and I
  think mine looks pretty bright!

By using common sense and thinking it through, I guessed cor-
rectly and came up smelling like a rose. And you can, too. Try your
luck with the following terms:

Penny stock: A stock in any company involved in the manufactur-
  ing and distribution of pennies.

Market top: That balcony above the New York Stock Exchange
  where they ring that big bell.

Spread: The free bagels, donuts, etc., available at investment seminars held at the Ramada Inn.

Bearish: The physique day traders eventually develop as a result of
  spreads.

Dip: Anyone who hires a stockbroker.

Swing trade: Strategy for adding spice to one's marriage, popularized
  in the novels of John Updike; also called "swapperooni."

EBITDA: Nonsense word used by Pebbles Flintstone.

Churning: Common day trader's stomach complaint.

Standard deviation: An obsession with ladies' high heels or hosiery.

Think it through. It's easy and it's fun. And remember, even if you're not always right about the terminology, you will still succeed if you know the meaning of the four most important words in day trading: "mouse," "point," "click," and "pizza."

That's all you need to know in order to "talk the talk." The obsessive among you may still feel that you need to know more and will search through musty old business texts to find the meaning of terms like "P/E ratio," "ex-dividend," and "basis point." If you find out what these words mean, please let me know.

PRINCIPLE NUMBER TWO

Select Stocks Carefully

I never buy stock in a company I've never heard
of, so I try to hear of thousands of new
companies every day.

—Carmine Bozell, day trader

Perhaps the most critical dilemma facing any day trader, with the possible exception of deciding whether his hair can go another day without shampooing, is determining which stocks to add to his portfolio.

As in every other aspect of day trading, these decisions must be governed by disciplined, scientific rules. These rules of stock selection apply equally to all industry groups: automotive companies, like Ford and General Motors, or chipmakers, like Intel and Frito-Lay.

I should remind you, at this juncture, that day trading is not the same thing as gambling. You're not betting on stocks. You're betting on *yourself*—and yourself is betting on stocks.

The "Name Game"

It was William Shakespeare who said, "What's in a name? Everything, when it comes to choosing stocks." Often, when novice investors are attempting to do "research" on a stock, they will breeze right past the name of the stock and delve into obscure and mind-numbing data like profits, cash flow, earnings projections, etc. In other words, they are making the understandable but foolish "beginner's mistake" of putting the cart before the horse—because nine times out of ten, *the most important information about a stock is contained in the name of the stock itself.*

That old shopworn adage "you can't judge a book by its cover" does not apply to stocks, and for a very simple reason: Stocks do not have covers.

How can you tell whether or not to buy a stock based on its name? Let's start with some simple examples.

Some Simple Examples

Recently, there has been a profusion of high-flying stocks beginning with the small letter "e" or ending with a "dot" and the letters "com"; the stocks ending "dot-com" are often referred to, among experienced day traders, as "dot-com" stocks. Sometimes you will even see stocks that begin with "e" *and* have a "dot-com" at the end.

What do "e" and "dot-com" mean? Doesn't matter. But one thing's for sure: *All of these stocks have something to do with the Internet.*

Now here's the beauty part—you don't have to do any more research, because you already know all you need to know in order to make your decision: *Buy these stocks as soon as possible.*

How can I be so confident in making this recommendation? For this simple, time-tested reason: Internet stocks always—and I mean *always*—go up.

I'm sure that the skeptics among you will put this book down and race for your newspaper's business section, looking to prove me wrong. In my opinion, that's a very rude, jerky thing to do. Sit down and keep reading. I'm talking to you.

After facing years of skepticism, Internet stocks have carried the day, and even Wall Street professionals, those notoriously dimwitted slow pokes, have started gobbling up stocks that have "e" and "dot-com" in them. And yet some skeptics persist. Read this excerpt, taken from one of our country's most respected business journals:

> Many unanswered questions remain about the stocks of Internet companies. Where will earnings and, ultimately, profits, come from? Even some of the best-established Internet companies have yet to show a profit. I know I'm a douchebag and I'm usually wrong, but I'm pretty sure I'm right about this.

Okay, I'll admit it—I didn't really find that excerpt in a business journal. I wrote it myself, after I had a couple of long-necked beers. But you'd be surprised just how much it's like something that one of those so-called experts *would* write.

Instead of scaring you with a bunch of data about "earnings" and "profits" that no one can understand anyway, I'm going to take an example from real life.

Let's say there's a town called Hypotheticalville, USA. In this town, there are two restaurants. Restaurant A is always empty, with just a lonely old waiter wiping down the counter and looking mournfully out at the street as people pass the place by, never going in.

Restaurant B is always packed with hot-looking women and buff guys. It's so popular that people push and shove each other to get in. There are fistfights and blood and people getting their asses kicked.

You always see ambulances pulling up to Restaurant B to rush all of the injured people to the hospital.

Which restaurant would you invest in? If you answered B, you're right.

By now, I think I've made my point: The Internet, like a restaurant where people are getting hurt and taken away in ambulances, is the place where everyone wants to be. Shouldn't you, and your money, be there, too?

Some More Examples

Amazon.com, America Online, and Amgen have been three of the stock market's biggest success stories over the past decade. What do these stocks have in common? They all begin with the letters "Am." Using history as my guide, I recommend the following stocks for every day trader's portfolio:

- Amalgamated Toxic Spilling

- American Lint Supply

- Amorouschimps.com

Even More Examples

Microsoft, Cisco Systems, Sun Microsystems, and Advanced Micro Devices have all zoomed in price over the last few years, and little wonder: They all have the words "micro" or "systems" in them. Be on the lookout for new stock offerings that contain either of these words: These stocks will always go up, big time.

A stock that I truly believe in is "e.systemsmicro.com," but so far no one has issued a stock called that yet. Like many day traders, I believe that it will happen someday—it is simply a matter of being a patient investor.

What is a "system"? What is a "microsystem"? You're asking the wrong hombre. It's safe to say that they both have something to do with technology. And I'll go out on a limb and say that a "microsystem" is probably smaller than a "system." But just how small *is* a microsystem? So small that it could be lost in shipping, or fall down a grate? You got me. Which leads me to another ironclad rule of stock selection: *Never own a stock long enough to know what the company does.*

I'm sure some of you will bristle at this notion. You'll say it is the duty of every investor, before he or she buys a stock, to know the company inside out, to know what it makes or what service it provides, and to know where it stands in its industry group.

With all due respect, that's why I'm writing this book, and you're just reading it.

The Myth of Knowing What a Company Does

It is someone's job to know what business a company is in—the CEO's, not the day trader's! Nothing steams me more than the idea that we, as day traders, are supposed to be spending all the livelong day trying to figure out what a company does, what its profits are, etc., while some lazy CEO calls it quits at five and hits the links with his martini-swilling pals.

As investors, we have demonstrated our faith in a company by tirelessly buying, selling, and buying it again twenty or thirty times in a given day. Consequently, we should *demand accountability* of these slacker CEOs and deliver the following message, loud and clear: *Hey, Mr. CEO—figure out what your company does, so we don't have to.*

I apologize for getting up on my soapbox, but this is one of those issues that really pisses me off.

The "Dartboard Portfolio"

Every so often, the *Wall Street Journal* publishes a feature in which a panel of so-called Wall Street experts is asked to put together theoretical portfolios of stocks. The results of these portfolios are then compared to a "dartboard portfolio": a portfolio assembled by throwing darts at a newspaper's stock listings mounted on a dartboard.

Surprisingly, the dartboard portfolio often yields better results than those designed by the Wall Street pros. What does this tell us?

A dartboard is an excellent way to choose stocks.

Now that you know about the dartboard system, how can you benefit from the same time-tested methodology used by the stock-market mavens of the *Wall Street Journal?* It's just a matter of getting started.

Getting Started

In your home office, hang a dartboard on the wall no closer than six feet away from your desk. Tape a line across the floor six feet from the dartboard, and remain behind the line as you hurl the darts. Remember, stepping over the line is cheating.

To resist the temptation to cheat, I remain seated at my desk, throwing darts with my left hand while operating the mouse with my right. This maximizes both throws and trades per minute, and eventually, with practice, I find myself getting into a nice "throw, point, click" rhythm.

THE DARTBOARD PORTFOLIO

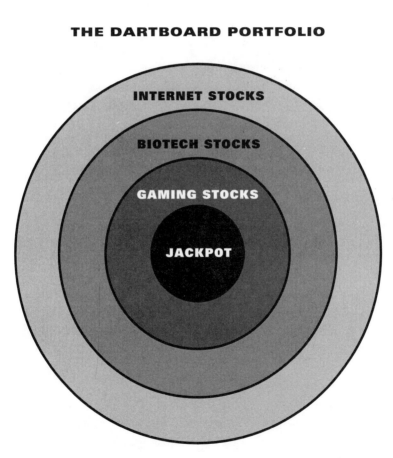

INTERNET STOCKS

BIOTECH STOCKS

GAMING STOCKS

JACKPOT

First Person:

NEIL HINTON

Neil Hinton left a key position behind the counter at Starbucks to become one of the pioneers—and true giants—of day trading. We happened to meet at a 7-Eleven, where we were both replenishing our Big Gulps and buying eye drops. For legal reasons, Neil's name, as well as a lot of the things that happened to him, have been changed.

—AB

I guess you could say I've always had kind of an obsessive personality. Not in any clinical sense, though—don't get me wrong. I mean, you read about people who wash their hands twenty, maybe thirty times a day—that's not me. Ever since I started day trading, I've gone days or weeks without washing my hands even once.

Still, being a day trader has made it difficult to do some of the things that other people are able to do, like have a relationship with a woman. My last girlfriend walked out on me because she thought I was spending too much of my time day trading. It's weird, too, because you didn't see me complaining about all of the weird hobbies *she* had—like "talking about her feelings."

In retrospect, I probably shouldn't have tried to check that Instinet quote during sex, but hindsight makes geniuses of us all, doesn't it?

The Longest Time

The longest I ever stayed at my screen without stopping was seventy-four hours. I was heading toward hour number seventy-five when I got a call from my dad—my Uncle Buddy had just passed away, and the funeral was going to be the next day.

I didn't know Uncle Buddy well, but I had always been told that he was a very wealthy man. I was sad to hear the news of his passing, and this is where the stereotypes about day traders being "greedy" have got it all wrong. Most non-day traders are thrilled to hear that a rich uncle has passed away—but when you're a successful day trader, you're your *own* dead rich uncle.

Anyway, my dad really wanted me to make the funeral, so I decided I'd wrap things up, catch a few hours of sleep, maybe take a shower, and go pay my respects.

Eighteen hours later, I was still at my screen, trading a hot IPO called DomGen, a company that was making gene-splicing technology available for home use. I didn't know anything about gene-splicing, or genes for that matter, but after a few hours of trading the stock I had become something of an expert in the field.

I was down about six dollars a share when I looked at the clock: Uncle Buddy's funeral was in forty-five minutes. I traded for another twenty minutes, then shut down.

Away from My Screen

It was gloomy and overcast that day, although, to be honest, it might have been bright and sunny—I don't pay a lot of attention to the weather. I must've been one of the last people to show up at the funeral, because by the time I got there, there was no parking left. I wound up parking way up on this hill overlooking the funeral home, and it was only when I got out of my car that I realized: I was still wearing my pajama top.

I hoped maybe nobody would notice, but if they gave me some strange looks, I realized, hey, that's their problem—at least I showed up.

A Crisis

During the funeral, though, I was kind of sorry I *did* show up. One of Uncle Buddy's friends was delivering a eulogy, and he kept referring to Uncle Buddy by his real name—"Gene." Every time he said the name "Gene" I could only think of one thing: gene-splicing, as in, my stake in DomGen. I checked my Palm VII and got the current price: I was up four dollars a share! Now was the time to dump my position—but how?

I had purposefully left my laptop in my car, out of respect for Uncle Buddy's wife, Aunt Estelle, but now I realized how dumb I had been. I had to get out of the funeral chapel as quickly as possible—and then get out of that stock.

I quickly came upon a solution. I started fake crying—just bawling my head off, making it look like I was overcome with emotion. I think I was pretty convincing, too, because people turned their heads to stare, and you could tell from the looks on their faces that they thought something was really wrong with me. I excused myself and ran out. Mission accomplished, and no one was the wiser.

People always used to tease me about fitting my car with a satellite uplink for easy Internet access, but it was emergencies like this that made my investment seem well worth it, and then some. I logged on and found that DomGen was up seven, and so I quickly dumped my entire stake.

Whenever I have a successful trade like that one, I go through a little ritual I call "the dump and pump." I dump the stock, then pump my fist in the air and say, "Yes!" That's exactly what I did this time, only my elbow must have come down on the emergency brake, because my car started rolling downhill.

Not What You Want to Happen

My car wound up landing in some kind of pond in the cemetery. The fire department had to come to fish me out, but I got out of my car alive, and my laptop was okay, too.

I remember looking up and seeing all of the funeral guests gathered around the fire truck, just kind of giving me the hairy eyeball. Aunt Estelle looked really pissed, but I thought at the time that maybe it was just grief.

A few weeks later, my dad told me that Aunt Estelle had cut me out of her will. He said she was mad at me for what went down at Uncle Buddy's funeral, but I'm not so sure. She probably just figured that since I'm a day trader, I'm already rich.

PRINCIPLE NUMBER THREE

Understand Valuations

Never pay more for a stock than you think it's worth, unless it comes recommended by someone you trust, like your UPS driver.

—Frances Dowling, day trader

We are a nation of consumers, well versed in the fine art of buying stuff. We think nothing of plunking down our hard-earned cash for a pair of socks, a magazine, or a six-pack of beer, and we have an innate sense of the price we are willing to pay for these items. And yet, when it comes to knowing what price to pay for a small-cap tech stock with several new patents pending in the field of microrobotics, we suddenly freeze. Why?

The fact is, if we know what to pay for *things*—like pants or beer—we should know what to pay for a stock, because, when all is said and done, a stock is a thing.

The Right Price Versus the Wrong Price

When it comes to a stock's price, how much is too much? And when is too much not enough? Let's listen in on a conversation between two successful day traders, overheard at the annual convention of the National Association of Successful Day Traders, held last May at the Lucky Seven Casino in Reno, Nevada:

DAY TRADER #1: I just bought a new stock.
DAY TRADER #2: Really? How much did you pay for it?
DAY TRADER #1: Thirty-five dollars a share.
DAY TRADER #2: Hey, that's a good price!

What can we take away from this exchange? A nugget of information so important to the budding day trader, I urge you to copy it down right now and commit it to memory: *The right price to pay for any share of stock is thirty-five dollars.*

At first blush, thirty-five dollars may seem like an arbitrary price, but it's not at all. Let's take a look at an example from real life.

If you went to the corner store and there were two six-packs of beer, one costing $5.99 and the other costing $11.99, you'd laugh at the notion of paying the higher price—because a six-pack is always worth $5.99, unless it's imported.

The same is true of buying stock. When you start to buy a stock, don't be intimidated: Pretend that you're buying a six-pack of beer. The "beer method" of stock valuation will take a great deal of the mystery out of the process and vastly improve your returns. Let's put it into action, shall we?

"Bid" Versus "Ask"

When you "bid" on a share of stock, pay close attention to the "ask" price, and then "ask" yourself—is the stock really worth it? Let's say the "ask" price is one hundred twelve dollars and thirteen-sixteenths. Take a deep breath, and think: If I went to the store to buy beer and they asked me to pay one hundred twelve dollars and thirteen-sixteenths for it, would I go for it? Of course you wouldn't—so don't buy the stock at that price either.

A good rule of thumb: If the ask price for the stock you are bidding on is well over thirty-five dollars, go out and buy beer instead. In the long run, beer will prove to be a better investment. Another tip: Nachos are good with beer, and bean dip is excellent with nachos.

Remember, there are other investment options out there besides just buying and selling stocks. To name just one: If the ask price for a share of stock is well over thirty-five dollars, click onto an online auction site, like eBay, and see what thirty-five dollars will buy you over there.

Oftentimes you will find something being auctioned online that is much more valuable than a dumb old overpriced stock. Do you own an action figure of Vanilla Ice that says "Ice, ice, baby," when you squeeze its waist? How about a shower cap that was once used by Ally Sheedy? Don't mean to brag, but I do.

If there is nothing of interest on eBay, remember that there are still other ways that an astute day trader can put his money to work. For example, it is now possible to buy supermodels' eggs online. These eggs may turn out to be the best investment option of all, since the world has a limited supply of supermodels, and therefore a limited supply of supermodel eggs. Prices vary from supermodel to supermodel, but be prepared to pay well over thirty-five dollars.

At the end of the day, if there are no stocks to be bought at a decent price, I'd consider it time well spent if I wound up with a six-pack of beer, some nachos, and some supermodel eggs instead. The key to success as a day trader is *flexibility.*

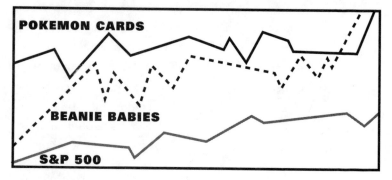

ALTERNATIVE INVESTMENT OPTIONS

POKEMON CARDS

BEANIE BABIES

S&P 500

Put Momentum to Work

When you've been riding the mo up and down
all day, and it's so nerve-wracking that you
think you're going to throw up—it doesn't get
any better than that.

—Rick Vermillion, day trader

Throughout the corridors of power in the old-line investment firms of Wall Street, "momentum investor" is a harsher epithet than "bed-wetter"—and yet, among day traders, just the opposite is true.

Why the disparity? Simple: "Momentum investing" is one of those concepts that smart people have trouble grasping but day traders don't.

Let's take a look at the word *momentum* itself, taken from the Latin words *mo,* meaning "more," and *mentum,* meaning "to mint money." In short, the word *momentum* means "mo' money."

Critics say that momentum investors are know-nothing lemmings, blindly following the latest half-baked NASDAQ stock off the nearest available cliff. To this allegation I humbly respond, "Guilty as charged." And yet, I have made *trillions* by throwing caution to the wind and jumping on the bandwagon—and you can, too.

As anyone who has ever been in a Labor Day parade knows, there's no harm in jumping on a bandwagon. It's the people who jump *off* the bandwagon who twist their ankles and break their necks. The same applies to the business of day trading: Those who are leery of momentum investing could be seriously injured and laid up in the hospital for weeks.

How do you put the power of "mo' money" to work for you? It's a simple matter of obeying the following rule:

Buy Stocks That Go Up, Not Ones That Go Down

If you buy stocks that go up, you will make money in the stock market; conversely, if you buy stocks that go down, you are far more likely to lose money than to make it. As simple as this may sound, you would be surprised how many novice day traders jump right into the market and, ignoring this wisdom, buy stocks that go down!

The trick, of course, is knowing which stocks go up and which ones go down. How can you tell which are which? Answer: On your screen, the stocks going up are in *green* letters. Buy them. The ones going down are in *red* letters. Do not buy them.

Easy way to remember: *green = up, red = down.* I recommend posting this "color guide" somewhere near your computer screen for the first few weeks of trading until you get the hang of it.

Sometimes a day trader will buy a stock that is going up and later notice that it is going down. At that point, he may find himself saying, "Hey, what's going on here?" Before he does, however, he should ask himself: Before I bought this stock, did I check to see if it had the letters "e" or "dot-com" in it? Does the name of the stock begin with the letters "Am"? The problem of stocks going down can often be avoided if the day trader has done his homework properly.

The issue of "up-and-down-ness," then, is critical to momentum investing. A stock either goes up or it goes down—but can it get more complicated than that?

It Can Get More Complicated Than That

At a recent investment seminar I held at an offshore post office box, three day traders reported to me some problems they were having with so-called unpredictable stocks: stocks that are capable of not just going up, but of going down, too. Here are the scenarios they described to me:

- Stock went up, then up some more, then went down, then went up, then went down.

- Stock went up, then down, then down some more, then went up, then went down.

- Stock went up, down, up, down, down, further down, way down.

Clearly, these stocks were flashing from red to green more often than the lights on a funky Christmas tree. Their behavior was completely volatile, random, and unpredictable.

Or was it?

The Myth of Unpredictability

Like any other science, day trading has no room for vague phenomena like unpredictability. I felt that the "myth of unpredictability" was the stuff of superstition and voodoo, and I sought to blow its lid off by applying scientific rigor. With the help of Alfred T. Hough, an economist who was wait-listed at Stanford University, I developed a schematic diagram that I call "The Tree of Up and Down." By using The Tree, the day trader can predict *exactly* the movement of any stock he invests in (see diagram, page 45).

I urge the serious investor to post a copy of The Tree near his computer screen, or better yet, commit it to memory.

One final thought about the issue of "up" versus "down." There is one—and only one—thing that will guarantee a stock's future results: *past performance.* You can take that to the bank.

Piling In, Bailing Out

If momentum investors all buy the same stock at the same time— because they notice that it is green—the stock will go up and up and up. If, however, the stock starts going down, they may all decide to bail out of the stock at the same time. If everyone "rushes for the exits" en masse, the stock will plummet and your investment in it will be wiped out.

Just kidding! This sort of doomsday scenario is just the kind of "old wives' tale" that is disseminated for one reason and one reason alone—to give day traders the willies. Who's behind these spooky stories? You guessed it: "The Man."

Don't Catch a Falling Knife

Tomes of literature about momentum investing often include the caveat "Don't catch a falling knife." This ominous-sounding piece of advice is really just a matter of common sense. Caught up in the

THE TREE OF UP AND DOWN

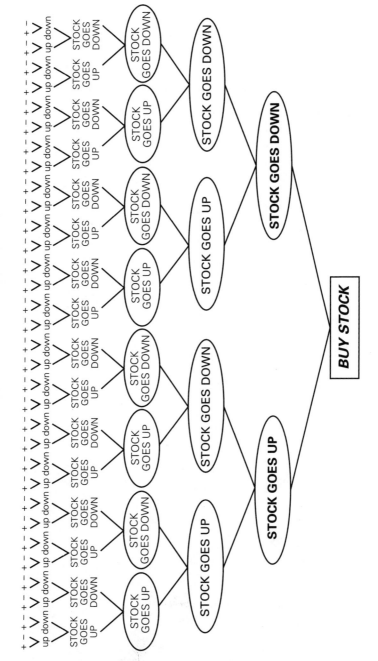

excitement of momentum investing, the day trader may make the mistake of leaving the knife he uses to slice his pizza at the edge of his desk, where it can easily fall if jostled. If it falls, don't try to catch it—you could cut yourself, or worse. Remember, investing is important, but your safety comes first.

CARRIE SLOCUM

No book about day trading, no matter how super-ficial, would be complete without mentioning the veteran day trader Carrie Slocum. At thirty-seven, she is still day trading—a full ten years past the age when most traders burn out and move into tele-marketing or phone sex. I asked her what the secret to her longevity was, but she said it was a secret.

—AB

Believe it or not, at first I was a little leery of day trading. Not because I thought I'd lose money or anything—I'd seen all of the commercials on TV that showed how easy it was, so I knew that los-ing money was impossible. No, I had another reason for being leery.

You see, I really like watching television during the day. That's when all of my favorite programs are on: *Leeza, Judge Judy, Jerry Springer*—especially *Jerry Springer*. I didn't think it was a good idea to day trade *and* watch TV at the same time—I figured I would wind up doing neither of them well. What if I was chanting "Jer-ry, Jer-ry, Jer-ry," along with the studio audience, and I accidentally clicked my mouse and bought the wrong stock? That wouldn't be good!

Friends of mine said, "Why don't you just tape your favorite shows with your VCR?" And I thought, *Yeah, that would solve my problem—if I knew how to* work *the darn thing.*

Then I found out about after-hours trading, and that changed everything.

Day Trading the Night Away

I guess you shouldn't call it "day trading" when it's in the middle of the night, but that's what I started doing. It's more peaceful during the wee hours of the morning, and except for the married couple in the apartment next door arguing about whether or not her mother is sucking money from them like a vampire-bat, it's pretty quiet, too.

When I started, I would just put a big pot of coffee on, trade until six in the morning, catch some shut-eye, and be awake in time to see *Ricki Lake* at one in the afternoon. I don't mean to gloat, but it was pretty much a dream existence.

Then something really weird happened.

The Really Weird Thing That Happened

One night I woke up and found myself at my computer screen. I checked the clock—it was four-thirty in the morning. I came to a creepy realization—I had fallen asleep in the middle of a trade. I checked my account to make sure that the trade had been exe-cuted—and that's when I noticed the *truly* weird thing. There had been between twenty and thirty trades in the last hour, and that could mean only one thing: *I had been day trading in my sleep.*

I'd never heard of anything like this. Well, okay, I knew that people could walk in their sleep or talk in their sleep, but trading stocks in your sleep seemed pretty freaky to me. Nervously, I went through the trades to make sure I hadn't been completely wiped out. That's when I noticed something even weirder—I had made a profit of six thousand dollars in my sleep!

I chalked the whole thing up to good luck and was grateful that my portfolio hadn't gotten killed in this spooky little episode. I remember thinking to myself, "Hope that never happens again!"

The Next Really Weird Thing

It happened again the next night. Now you can imagine I'm *completely* freaking out. I'm even thinking that maybe I should go on *Jerry Springer* and ask him and the studio audience for help with my problem. But then I realized that to get on the show I would probably have to pretend to be sleeping with a relative or a goat or something, so I decided against it.

Then I added up the trades for that night and realized that while I was asleep I had made another *eight* thousand dollars.

Weird.

What I Learned

This went on for another two weeks or so, so I decided to do a little experiment. I tallied up all of my profits for day trading when I was awake and when I was asleep. Here were the results:

- Awake: −12 percent

- Asleep: +78 percent

There was no question about it. I was a much better day trader unconscious than I was conscious. It was hard to swallow at first, but as any good day trader will tell you, in this business you really have to check your ego at the door.

CONTROLLING YOUR EMOTIONS

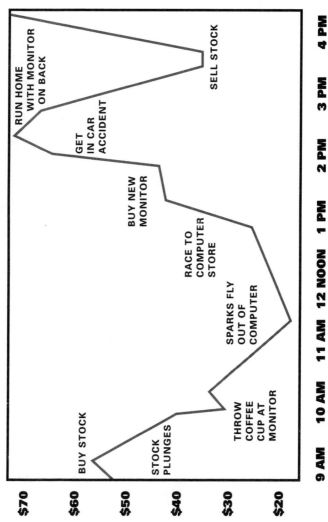

PRINCIPLE NUMBER FIVE

Get the Best Advice

I only take advice from myself, and half the
time I don't listen to that.

—Franklin Knepper, day trader

When it comes to the science of day trading, sometimes it seems as though everybody's an expert these days.

Hardly a week goes by that some know-it-all you've never heard of comes out with a line of day trading infomercials, how-to books, and even edu-tainment cassettes, all full of unhelpful, contradictory information.

At times like this, it can get a little hard to tell the forest from the trees. So where does a day trader go for information he can trust?

Some would recommend that the best way to understand the movements of the markets would be by consulting the writings of the greatest economists in history. Their works, these people would argue, have stood the test of time and are much more helpful to the day trader than the latest scam artist's 112-page book could ever be. This argument makes a great deal of sense.

Or does it?

The Myth of the Great Economists

The only way to assess the value of the classics of economic theory is by going to your nearest bookstore, superficially flipping through them, having a latte, and leaving without buying any of them. Fortunately for you, I have already gone through this exercise, so you don't have to.

Let's take Adam Smith's *The Wealth of Nations,* published in 1776, exactly two hundred years before Elton John recorded the classic anthem "Philadelphia Freedom." The jacket copy tells us that Mr. Smith's book is the foundation for all modern economics. Surely, then, his book must be chock-full of good advice for the day trader. Let's sneak a peek:

> The drought in Bengal, a few years ago, might probably have occasioned a very great dearth. Some improper regulations, some injudicious restraints imposed by the servants of the East India Company upon the rice trade, contributed, perhaps, to turn that dearth into a famine.

Say what? I didn't see anything in there about "pointing," "clicking," or any of the other things day traders do, did you? But maybe he wrote that passage on an off day. Let's give my man Adam a second chance and check out another passage:

> Bordeaux is in the same manner the entrepot of the wines which grow upon the banks of the Garonne, and of the rivers which run into it, one of the richest wine countries in the world, and which seems to produce the wine fittest for exportation, or best suited to the taste of foreign nations.

Well, it's nice to know that Mr. Adam Smith enjoys his wine— and it certainly *explains* a lot, if you know what I mean. But I'm still not finding anything in *The Wealth of Nations* that seems even remotely helpful to day traders. Okay, let's give him one last shot: Let's look up "mousepad" in the book's index. Nope, nothing there—and the closest thing I can find is "Mosaical law of inheritance in New England":

> In three of the provinces of New England the oldest has only a double share, as in the Mosaical law. Though in those provinces, therefore, too great a quality of land—

And now I think it's time to close the book on old Adam Smith. When I read "classics of economics" like this, I just get mad: What kind of suckers do these con men think we are?

Economists You Can Trust a Lot

But let's not let the example of Adam Smith leave a bad taste in our mouths about all economists; as the saying goes, "One bad apple don't spoil the whole bunch, girl." There are plenty of living, breathing economists whose knowledge towers above that of Mr. Smith.

At the top of any list of contemporary economists, one name soars above all the rest: CNN's Willow Bay. Ms. Bay has overcome many obstacles in her career, including having a name that makes people confuse her with a body of water, to become one of the most highly respected economic thinkers in the world today.

Unlike most economists, who spew streams of incomprehensible, inapplicable theory and are almost always wrong, Willow Bay makes clear, honest predictions—and she's always right. Take a look at the following example, from a recent outing of hers on CNN's *Moneyline* program:

Willow Bay: Now let's take a look at today's numbers from NASDAQ.

And within seconds, the numbers from NASDAQ appeared onscreen—just the way she called it.

Willow Bay, or that old drunk Adam Smith. The choice is yours.

Why Stockbrokers Don't Know Anything

Here are two things that stockbrokers really like to do:

1. Laugh in their customers' faces about how much money they're making on the poor saps' commissions.

2. Smugly chuckle as they drive up to the front door of their huge mansions—paid for by their idiotic customers' commissions.

How do I know that stockbrokers do these things? I've seen them do it, time and time again, in all of those TV commercials for online trading services. And yet, as puzzling as it may seem, some people still continue to hire stockbrokers.

Why do they do it?

Quite simply, it doesn't make sense. After all, if stockbrokers knew so much about investing money, wouldn't they be investing *their* money instead of *yours?*

Think about it. You have an idea of a hot stock to invest in—what's the first thing you do? Call up somebody you barely know and just give the tip away, or use it yourself and become a trillionaire?

Let's put it another way. To use an analogy from the world of cockfighting, let's say that you know one of the cocks in the ring is a champion bird who is going to peck the other bird's head off. Would you place a bet on the champion bird, or would you turn to the fellow next to you and say, "You know, I'm not really interested in making any money today—why don't you place a bet on that bird and get really rich?"

Replace the words "you" with "stockbroker," "guy next to you" with "stockbroker's customer," and "champion bird" with "hot stock that the stockbroker recommended to you instead of to himself," and perhaps you'll get some idea of what I'm talking about.

The reason stockbrokers make money collecting commissions rather than investing their own money in the "great" stocks they pick is that *they don't have the slightest idea what they're doing when it comes to picking stocks.*

Remember, if stockbrokers were as smart as day traders, they'd be day traders.

You may ask, how have stockbrokers gotten away with this scam for so long? It's amazing, I agree, but then again, it took over two hundred years for people to catch up with that sneaky bastard Adam Smith.

Stockbrokers, I'm sure, will object to my portrayal of them in these pages. Yes, the truth hurts, but that's why "truth" is "hurts" spelled backward—practically.

Warren Buffett: "Oracle of Omaha" or Just a Big Knucklehead?

Every year thousands of investors in Berkshire Hathaway descend on Omaha, Nebraska, for the company's annual meeting, a chance to hear the company's founder, legendary investor Warren Buffett, share his secrets for investment success. Inevitably, Buffett tells them the same thing: Buy good stocks and hold them forever, and you will make money.

To this so-called wisdom, I respond, "Duh!" That's not investing—that's a coma. For those of you who enjoy watching grass grow, paint dry, and opera, Warren Buffet's your man. As a day trader, though, I don't have all day.

Who to Trust

When all is said and done, there is only one consistently reliable source of stock-market information for the day trader: Internet chat rooms. Full of knowledgeable experts who have nothing else going on in their lives but online investing, Internet chat rooms are as invaluable to a day trader as a banana is to a chimp.

Having said this, it is important to recognize that not all participants in the chat room are equally well versed in the complex science of investing. Therefore, you should always follow the advice of people with intelligent-sounding screen names, like Marketguru, Knowsalot, and Swifty. Ignore advice from people with screen names like Bonehead, Howdoyouworkthisthing, and Beatsme.

Much has been written about people gaining access to a chat room for the purpose of "hyping" or "trashing" a stock or otherwise spreading misinformation for their own personal gain. The danger of this occurring has been vastly overstated—largely because the other chatters are usually so darn smart, they can smell a phony from a mile away. The following transcript from one recent chat I listened in on illustrates my point.

HOTPICKS: I just bought shoelaces.com at eleven, but it isn't doing nothing.

SMARTYPANTS: Buy more then. It'll go up.

HOTPICKS: Okay.

WORRYWART: I wonder what the Fed's going to do.

HOTPICKS: You mean FedEx?

WORRYWART: No, I mean the Federal Reserve.

HOTPICKS: What the hell you talkin about?

WORRYWART: Tomorrow's the meeting of the Open Market Committee. If they raise the discount rate, I think it could adversely affect the market.

HOTPICKS: You don't know what you talkin about!!! Shut the *hell* up!!!!

SMARTYPANTS: Yeah!!! Get the *hell* out of this *damm* room!!!!

As you can see, the technique known as "flaming"—providing insightful criticism of another chatter's irrelevant remarks—helps filter out extraneous or misleading "noise" and keeps the chat room's discussion on point.

Which stock-market chat rooms are the best? They are all excellent, but I invite you to log on to my site, www.sexytrillionaire.com. In addition to real-time quotes, hot stock tips, and news you can use, it has the most extensive lists of Carmen Electra and Pamela Anderson Lee links on the Internet today.

Understand the Markets

It's a tricky business trying to predict whether
the market will go up or down. That's why it's a
lucky thing that it just goes up.

—Sharon Buell, day trader

Hardly a day goes by that a stock-market commentator doesn't say something about "market psychology" or "market sentiment." This, like so much of the information available to the day trader, is totally bogus.

In order to have "psychology," the market would have to have a brain. And in order to have "sentiment," the market would have to have a heart. But like two famous fellow-travelers on the Yellow Brick Road to Oz, the Tin Man and the Scarecrow, the stock market has neither.

Don't take my word for it. Take a close look at the New York Stock Exchange the next time you see it on TV. You'll see a big board and a stock ticker, you'll see a big floor and a balcony with a bell on it, but you won't see a heart or a brain. Therefore, all discussion of "market psychology" and "market sentiment" is strictly for the gullible dope. Does that describe you? I didn't think so!

Now that I have convincingly proved my point about market psychology and sentiment, you are probably asking yourself: If these things do not exist, how does one predict the movement of the markets?

Outsmarting a Random Market

Perhaps the best way to outwit a random market is by behaving even more randomly and erratically than the market does. It's only common sense: The weirder and more unpredictable your behavior becomes, the more you'll keep the market guessing, instead of the market keeping *you* guessing.

What kind of erratic, random behavior do I encourage you to engage in? Here are some examples:

- When you mean to buy a stock, sell it.

- When you mean to sell a stock, buy it.

- When you mean to short a stock, fix yourself a snack.

- Make a lot of jerky, spasmodic motions with the mouse that have no intended result whatsoever.

Keep up a steady program of this random behavior, and I think you'll be delighted with the results. Remember, when it comes to this "random" stuff, the market started it—you're just giving the market a taste of its own medicine. See how much the market likes *your* random behavior—and watch it cry "uncle."

The Magic of Market Timing

Another way a day trader can accurately jump in and out of a choppy market is through a disciplined program of market timing. The way market timing works is actually quite simple. You go through all of the past records of the stock market's performance, run the data through a computer, and then get a printout that tells you the months, days, and times that the stock market always goes up.

By working closely with Eugene Burkett, an economist who for many years applied to Harvard University, I was able to synthesize the data necessary to time the market with 100 percent accuracy—*or better.* The following, then, is a list of months in which the stock market *always* goes up:

- January

- May

- June

- August

- October

Some of you may ask, "Didn't the stock market crashes of 1929 and 1987 happen in October?" That is correct, but let us remember: Both of those crashes occurred before day trading was even invented.

Moving on, the market always goes up on these dates:

- 2nd

- 4th

- 5th

- 9th

- 11th

- 12th

- 21st

- 27th

- 30th

You may ask, "If the market always goes up on the 30th, what do I do in February, which only has twenty-eight days?" The answer? Go to the beach—because, if you'll notice, February isn't on the list of "good" months. As you can see, this system is absolutely airtight—the kind of system that only an irritating wise guy would question.

Finally—and perhaps most important—the following are the *times of day* that the market always goes up:

- 9:47

- 10:03

- 10:21

- 11:08

- 11:12

- 11:42

- 12:06

- 12:09

- 1:32

- 1:38

- 1:45

- 2:09

- 2:49

- 3:01

- 3:26

- 3:51

I strongly recommend that every day trader commit these times of day to memory. All times are Eastern Standard Time (EST), except for one of them.

Understanding the "Elliot Wave" Model

The so-called Elliot Wave is a mathematical model that can be very useful to traders in predicting the movements of the stock market.

Have you ever hit yourself in the head repeatedly with a big wooden bat? I have, and trust me—that's how much your head is going to hurt if you spend even ten seconds trying to understand the Elliot Wave. Let's move on.

Mastering the Monetary System

One final skill of utmost importance to any day trader trying to understand the markets is a firm grasp of the monetary system.

Here's how the monetary system works. Take some money out of your pocket and throw it up in the air. If it's "heads," the market will go up; if it's "tails," the market will go down. By carefully applying this system, the day trader has a 50 percent chance of being right— and as any serious investor knows, 50 percent is an excellent rate of return.

Control Your Emotions

I try not to take this business personally, but
some of my stocks are really out to get me.

—Martha McHale, day trader

In a recent survey, a random sampling of Americans were asked who, in their opinion, was most likely to lose their cool and "go off." Day traders, unfortunately, ranked near the top of the list, along with postal workers and Latrell Spreewell of the New York Knicks.

The stereotype of the stressed-out day trader who flips out at the drop of a hat—or more accurately, at the drop of a NASDAQ stock called eHats.com—has been fanned by the news media, those notorious scavengers who are always looking for a sensationalistic angle.

Hollywood is part of the problem, too. I recently read that a movie studio is planning a film about a day trader starring none other than Robert De Niro, who has enchanted audiences with his memorable performances as a psycho in such films as *Taxi Driver*, *Cape Fear*, and *The Fan*. Yikes!

Even in movies when he's not playing a psycho, like the one where he was in love with Meryl Streep, you still get the feeling that he could snap at any minute and wring her Oscar-winning neck. I don't know about you, but I just can't wait to see his "balanced" portrayal of a day trader. Bet he has some cute catchphrase like "Limit *this*" and blows someone away in the first five minutes.

Like all stereotypes, the "psycho day trader" is based on half-truths and exaggerations and doesn't reflect the reality. What *is* the reality? For every two day traders who completely lose it and go on a psychotic rampage, there's another one who goes about his business peacefully and without incident. So much for the stereotype!

Still, the issue of controlling your emotions is crucial to you as a day trader, not because of the damage you might do to people or property, but because of the adverse effects a psychotic episode could have on your investment returns. It's natural for day traders to fall in and out of love with certain stocks, but when they start trying to marry and divorce their stocks, as some day traders have attempted to do, it's time for a reality check.

RECOMMENDED EMOTIONAL ALLOCATION

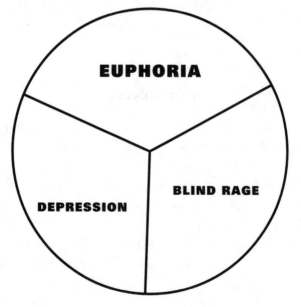

EUPHORIA

BLIND RAGE

DEPRESSION

"Winners" and "Losers"

Every night on CNBC, the network scrolls down a list of stock-market "winners" and "losers." The emphasis on winners versus losers is easy to get caught up in, especially when you own every one of the losers on a consistent basis. The day trader may fear that if his portfolio is full of losers, he may become a loser himself—the kind of person who is cruelly ostracized by his peers and cannot get a date on Saturday night. This fear, of course, is completely justified, since that is precisely what will happen.

Once a day trader recognizes that the losers in his portfolio have turned *him* into a loser, destined to spend many lonely evenings watching *Xena* reruns in his crummy apartment, he cannot be blamed for getting angry at his stocks. He may even start to take it out on them—shouting at them, cursing at them, and calling them childish names, like "dumb-ass" and "peckerwood." Believe me, I've been there.

If you shout obscenities at your stocks, does that mean you are becoming unhinged or psychotic? Absolutely not. Screaming at your stocks just shows that you have a healthy degree of interest in your investment portfolio. Similarly, it is not at all uncommon for a skilled day trader to throw things or to trash his computer. To be honest, I would be more concerned about a day trader who *didn't* do these things!

Scream at your losers, call them names, burn them in effigy. But there is one thing you must never do: *Never, ever sell them.*

This may seem like a paradox. Day traders often think, *This stock is killing my portfolio and making me lose a lot of money—shouldn't I dump it?* To the contrary, if a stock in your portfolio is in a free fall, the only sensible thing to do is to *buy as much of it as you can.*

Come Again?

It only stands to reason. A stock loses value when people start selling it. That's when it starts feeling like a "loser." Then it sees its name on the list of losers on CNBC every night—how's *that* supposed to make it feel? Remember, stocks are only human.

There's only one way to turn that "loser" into a "winner"—buy more shares!

You'll see how it works. Suddenly, now that you're buying it, the loser stock won't feel like such a loser anymore. The stock will feel a surge of confidence and start "strutting its stuff" up and down the stock market. As the loser in your portfolio gradually turns into a winner, you'll start turning into a winner, too. You'll start feeling better about yourself, and guess what? You'll even be more attractive to women.

Other Ways to Make a Stock Go Up

I'm often asked by perfectly intelligent people, "Will it help one of my stocks go up if I shout encouraging things at the screen, like, 'Come on, baby, go up, you can do it, baby, come on, come on, go up!'"

My answer to this line of inquiry is simple: *It couldn't hurt.*

Scientists have already proved beyond a shadow of a doubt the tremendous powers of psychic energy. If, as it has been shown, you can use psychic energy to bend a spoon or a fork, or to make a greyhound win a race, making a stock go up really shouldn't be a biggie. There are myriad examples of psychic powers contributing to a successful business venture, but let's take a look at just one: the Psychic Friends Network.

The Psychic Friends Network has earned millions of dollars in revenue and attracted the endorsements of experts in the field of psychic research, like Dionne Warwick. With credentials like these, it's no wonder that psychicfriendiology is now a widely recognized science, just like day trading.

To put it in layman's terms, saying encouraging things to your stocks will make them feel better and will make them want to perform better for you. Remember what it felt like when your boss told you that you had done a good job—way back when, when you still had a job? It made you feel good—in other words, it put you in an "up" mood, not a "down" one.

What makes you think your stocks would react any differently? Keep those kind words coming. And don't be afraid to kiss the screen from time to time—no one's looking.

Some naysayers no doubt will ask, "How is saying encouraging things to your computer screen any different from saying them to a roulette wheel?" I should remind those skeptical cranks, once again, that day trading is not the same thing as gambling. Having said that, however, it is only responsible to point out that saying nice things to a roulette wheel also works.

Ignoring Things That Are Annoying

One piece of advice I can't stress enough is to "stay focused"—don't get caught up in emotions that will distract you from your ultimate goal. One of these destructive emotions is envy—the "Green Monster," if I may coin a phrase.

Oftentimes a day trader makes the mistake of paying attention to how well *other* day traders are doing and getting trapped in a destructive cycle of competitiveness. Perhaps you have an irritating brother-in-law who, in addition to gloating about his stupid son's karate awards and his ugly daughter's ballet recitals, brags about his account being up 79 percent year-to-date—and then asks how *you're* doing. When confronted with a situation like this, you should do what I always do: Lie like a rug.

Rational Exuberance

Today, as I write this chapter, I've already made some eighty-four trades in my portfolio. I'm "in the zone" today, and everything I'm doing is coming out right—so right, in fact, that I'm already up a trillion dollars. On days like today, I feel as though my stocks are all going up forever and ever, and that the Dow will hit sixty thousand before the end of the year.

Well, guess what? *It will.*

That's right: Dow sixty thousand, *before the end of this year.* And if not this year, definitely next year. And if not next year, the year after that.

Irrational exuberance? Hardly. It's what I call "rational exuberance." Somebody who's got the Midas touch like me and *isn't* exuberant—now that's what I call irrational!

Let's look at another scenario. Your dry cleaner tells you about a new tech stock called Syntrontektrix. You race home, log on, skip the research page, and buy a thousand shares. It goes up. So you buy a thousand more shares. It goes up again. So you buy ten thousand shares. It goes up *again!* You start giggling and do an Irish jig around the room—and then a little hula.

Exuberance? Yes. Irrational? No.

Do you know what I call irrational? Statements like these: "Stocks don't go up in a straight line." Oh, they don't? "This bull market can't last forever." Oh, it can't? What are these statements based on? A certain "feeling" you have? You're making an investment call based on an irrational *feeling?*

Shame on you!

Do you know what a trillionaire calls somebody who invests using feelings as his guide?

A *millionaire.*

SMOKEY JOE MCDOUGAL

Smokey Joe McDougal is more than a day trader—
he's an entrepreneur, having founded one of the
first day trading shops in America, QuickyTrade of
St. Louis. As the competition among day trading
shops heated up, QuickyTrade became Quickier-
Trade, then QuickiestTrade. Today it is a tanning
salon, and Smokey Joe McDougal works at home.
I asked him how he got the name "Smokey Joe," to
which he replied, "I used to smoke. And before the
SEC investigators moved in, I used to be named
Joe."

–AB

I'm just a normal, run-of-the-mill day trader—I mean, nothing out
of the ordinary has ever happened to me. Well, maybe *one* thing.

When I started setting up my office at home, I wanted to make
sure there were no distractions. I painted the windows black and
installed soundproof carpet and ceiling tiles. It was so quiet you
could hear a pin drop. In fact, the only sounds in the room came

from the three television sets I always had on at the same time, tuned to CNNFN, CNBC, and Bloomberg.

I listened to all of the financial commentators, but I would have to say that my favorite by a mile was CNBC's "Money Honey," Maria Bartiromo. She was always up first thing in the morning, reporting from the floor of the New York Stock Exchange, and she was still hard at work at the end of the day, hosting *Market Wrap*. She seemed like the hardest-working person on Wall Street—with the exception of me maybe. I guess since we both kept about the same work hours, and we both were really serious about the stock market, I felt a special connection with Maria Bartiromo.

One day as she was running down the early action on the floor of the NYSE, I heard Maria Bartiromo say, "Internet stocks are leading this powerful rally, so now's the time to buy them, Smokey Joe." I stopped what I was doing and looked at the TV. I figured it must've been my imagination. Maria Bartiromo couldn't have been speaking to *me*. "You heard me—buy some Internet stocks," she said. "And by the way, you've got some Froot Loops on your bathrobe."

I checked my bathrobe, and sure enough, she was right.

How Do You Solve a Problem Like Maria Bartiromo

At first I thought maybe I had just been working too hard—after all, the mind can play tricks on you. But as the days passed, Maria Bartiromo continued to give me advice from the TV. "I think you're going to want to lighten up on Amazon, Smokey Joe," she would say—things like that. I recognized that this was all kind of unusual, but my trades were better than they had ever been, so I didn't question it. At the end of each day, I would just say good-bye to Maria Bartiromo, she would say good-bye to me, and that would be that.

The only problem was, that *wouldn't* be that. Over the weekends, when the markets were closed and I wasn't trading—and I didn't even have the TV on—I could still hear Maria Bartiromo talking to me. "You should think about moving, Smokey Joe," Maria Bartiromo would say to me, from somewhere inside my head. "This apartment is too small for us."

After a few weeks of this, I started to begin to feel as though Maria Bartiromo was playing too big a role in my life. I wanted to get things back to where they used to be, when she was just my favorite commentator and she wasn't telling me what shirt to wear in the morning, or that I was having too many Pop-Tarts.

I don't mean to say that she wasn't right—she was *always* right. I just wanted to tell her that I needed my own space. But I was afraid that if I told her anything like that, she might stop giving me stock tips. So I just kept my big mouth shut.

The Money Honey Pulls Something Funny

I decided I needed a break, though. Maybe if I spent a couple of weeks away from Maria Bartiromo, the breather would do us both good. So I clicked on priceline.com and bought a ticket to Paris. It was one of those bargain fares, with stops in St. Louis, Dallas, Iceland, and Helsinki.

At first, things in Paris were great. I visited the Arc de Triomphe, the Champs Elysées, all the sights you have to see when you visit there. For the first time in weeks, my head felt clear. Then, one day as I was walking through the Louvre museum, I heard a familiar voice: "Biotechs are rallying this morning, Smokey Joe, and you're missing out on the action." You guessed it: Maria Bartiromo.

I decided it was time to see a psychiatrist. I had hoped I could be psychoanalyzed over the Internet, where it might take less time away from my trading, so I logged on to www.jungiananalyst.com. The tech adviser, who turned out to be a sophomore psychology major at Tulane, said my case sounded really serious, and he advised me to see somebody in person. So I did.

As I lay on the "real" psychiatrist's couch, I found myself blurting out the truth: Maria Bartiromo was talking to me, day and night, giving me advice even when I didn't ask for it. At this point, the psychiatrist, who had seemed pretty uninterested, perked up. He leaned forward and said, "What does she think Yahoo is going to do?"

What I Learned

It was at that moment that I realized—I was *lucky* that Maria Bartiromo has decided to talk to me. Any other investor would gladly have traded shoes with me. Now, somebody who wanted Maria Bartiromo to *stop* talking to him—*that's* what I call a crazy person. I popped up from the psychiatrist's couch and never went back.

Things have calmed down since then. Maria Bartiromo still talks to me, although more some days than others, I guess depending on how busy she is. On a triple-witching Friday, for example, I'll get a "Good morning, Smokey Joe," out of her and that's pretty much it. Which is cool.

Why did she choose *me* to talk to? I guess I'll never know. The important thing is, *she* knows.

She knows everything.

Know Your Risk Tolerance

Sure, day trading is risky, but so are lots of
other things I do, like hang gliding and driving
with my eyes closed.

—Buster "Nutso" Heflin, day trader

In his famous song "The Day Trader," Kenny Rogers sings, "You've got to know when to hold 'em, know when to fold 'em." No truer words have ever been sung on the theme of risk tolerance, a critical issue for all day traders—whether they are trading trillion-dollar accounts or just next month's rent money.

Determining one's risk tolerance is like shopping for a mattress: What one person is comfortable with may give another person sleepless nights and lower back pain—and *good luck* trying to get the store to take the mattress back. So, before we determine your own personal level of risk tolerance, take a moment now to take the following Day Trader's Risk Tolerance Quiz:

Since you started day trading, have you experienced any of the following symptoms?

☐ Shortness of breath

☐ Hives

☐ Nervous twitches

☐ Unexplained chest pains

☐ Inability to digest food

☐ Screaming fits

☐ Stress-induced seizures

☐ Nightmares in which you are flayed and eaten alive by Alan Greenspan

☐ Loss of the will to live

If you answered yes to five or more of those symptoms, congratulations—you are well within the commonly recognized "comfort zone" necessary to prosper as a day trader.

The Miracle of Asset Allocation

For those of you with a lower risk tolerance, there's another way to stay in the day trading game without losing sleep or, as is often the case, shaking uncontrollably and relinquishing control of vital bodily functions. This technique is called "asset allocation."

It's simple, really. Nobody ever said you had to invest all of your money in your day trading account. By spreading your risk out among several different asset classes, you expose yourself to a lower level of risk and are much less likely to experience sudden, mysterious skin conditions. Here's an asset allocation model I recommend to those squeamish investors looking to "hedge their bets."

ASSET ALLOCATION MODEL

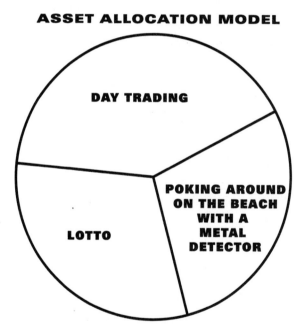

Start Slowly!

Another way to reduce your risk is by gradually backing into the market rather than jumping in all at once. To borrow an analogy from real life, day trading is like bullfighting. A novice bullfighter wouldn't dream of jumping into a ring alone with an angry, murderous bull—he always brings a gun with him. The same commonsense principle prevails here.

The following investment schedule is by no means "one size fits all," but it is intended to give you some idea of how to commit assets to your day trading account gradually without exposing yourself to unreasonable risks right from the get-go:

- Week One: Invest fifty dollars a day.

- Week Two: Invest one hundred dollars a day.

- Week Three: Invest one thousand dollars a day.

- Week Four: Sell car, invest proceeds.

- Week Five: Sell clothes, invest proceeds.

- Week Six: Invest grocery money, eat Ramen noodles.

It's that simple. And, of course, you can modify the schedule to your own level of risk tolerance. For example, if you own a house, you may want to leverage that asset. By "leverage" I mean, sell your house and its contents and invest the proceeds in a stock you just heard about ten minutes ago from the guy at the gas station.

How do you know when you are "fully invested"—in other words, when it is time to invest no more of your assets? On this question, the scientific principles of day trading speak loudly and clearly: You should stop investing once you have lost all of your money.

Maintain a Proper Diet

*I find that my trading improves if I do it with my
mouth full.*

—Dick Terrell, day trader

Maintaining a proper diet is a subject that is completely
ignored in all of the so-called authoritative and expert guides to day
trading, which is one of the reasons those books blow.

People scoff at the notion that day traders should have a diet
specifically designed for their profession. Why is this the case when
it is commonly accepted that football players, for example, should
eat a diet rich in protein and anabolic steroids, or that high fashion
models should feast on diet pills and laxatives?

There are three keys to creating a diet that will help you as a day
trader operate at peak performance:

1. Foods should be high in fats and oils, which help to lubricate the
   synapses in your brain.

2. Foods should be easy to shove in your mouth, enabling you to
   have your mouse-operating hand free at all times.

3. Foods should not go bad if left unrefrigerated on your desk for five days or more.

Given these simple rules, it's amazing how many day traders opt for odd dietary supplements, like "ginkgo" and "ginseng" and other so-called smart herbs. The manufacturers of these products boast that by taking them you will increase your mental sharpness and alertness. Hmm . . . it seems that there's another natural product out there that can do those things for me. I believe it's called "coffee."

When to Buy, When to Sell, When to Call Domino's

No discussion of a day trader's diet would be complete without a thorough discussion of pizza, nature's so-called wonder food. In addition to possessing the high levels of fat a day trader needs to keep his brain a "well-oiled machine," pizza is a day trader's secret weapon for another reason: The pizza delivery boy will often have excellent stock tips.

Sometimes I order a pizza when I'm not particularly hungry but I'm on the verge of putting through a major buy order and I want a knowledgeable and impartial adviser's input. Plus, if they show up late, they have to pay you—funds that can immediately be plowed back into your trading account.

Some skeptics will say that a diet rich in fats, while undeniably "smart" food, could lead to weight gain, heart problems, and other health difficulties for the day trader who, after all, spends many hours at his screen and does not get any exercise. And to be fair, these are legitimate concerns.

Or are they?

The Myth of Fat Being Bad for You Instead of Being Good for You

Here's the good news, Day Trader: Fat is your friend.

True, there might be some health risks involved in eating too many fats. But if you injected a gallon's worth of carrot juice or some other "health" food directly into your head, that would kill you, too.

THE IMPORTANCE OF DIET

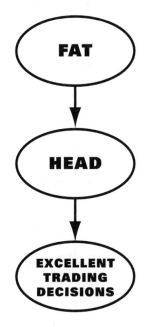

The biggest flaw in the anti-fat argument is that day traders "don't get any exercise." As any day trader knows, the average day is full of activity that is physically draining—clicking the mouse, turning up the volume on the remote, ordering pizza, throwing darts. It's a punishing workout. Spend a day being put through those kinds of paces and you'll see: An Olympic decathlete has nothing over today's active day trader.

Stick to the Diet and the Diet Will Stick to You

A day trader is only as smart as the food he eats. So if you want to be smarter, always eat food that is smarter than you are.

Sticking to any diet is hard, but the first step, of course, is education. By creating the Day Trader's Food Pyramid, I have provided the day trader with a simple guide to make sure that he's getting all of the good things he needs.

DAY TRADER'S FOOD PYRAMID

PRINCIPLE NUMBER TEN

Cope with Burnout

I'd like to day trade for another five years or so,
but unfortunately, I'm losing my eyesight.

—Eileen K. Larsen, day trader

I have saved the topic of day trading "burnout" for last because of
the taboo nature of this subject. Among day traders, burnout is truly
the affliction that "dares not speak its name."

Think I'm exaggerating? Hardly. If you get a bunch of day
traders together, you'll find that they are perfectly willing to discuss
the severe sexual dysfunction that is rampant among day traders, but
if you even mention the touchy topic of day trading burnout, they
just clam up. And yet it is only by bringing this unpleasant subject
out in the open that we, as day traders, can learn to deal with it.

In an ideal world, people could day trade for twenty, thirty years
or more. We would have legions of retirees day trading well into
their nineties instead of sitting around complaining about the
worthless bastards their daughters married. And yet, the sad fact is
that the average day trader's career lasts only 6.3 *months*. Why? In
some cases, the traders lose interest; in others, they become trillionaires and go on to write helpful, informative books. But in most
cases, they just plain burn out.

We all have heard about the common housefly who has a life span of twenty-four hours. To put things in perspective, if that housefly were a day trader, it would live only *half that long*. That is because the day trader has a much more stressful job than the fly, who, when all is said and done, just has to fly around the house.

The Miracle of Multitasking

One reason day traders get stressed out is that they find themselves feeling overwhelmed by other tasks that often go unattended for weeks, like paying bills, doing laundry, and brushing teeth. The day trader can relieve this burden, however, through the miracle of "multitasking": doing many jobs at once, and doing them all splendidly.

"Multitasking" comes from the Latin *multi,* meaning "many," and *taskus,* meaning "taskets." By multitasking, then, the day trader is able to accomplish a variety of jobs by placing them all in the same green and yellow basket.

Here's a quick multitasking quiz:

Which *two* of the following items can be done simultaneously?

- Day trading

- Folding laundry

- Exercising on a treadmill

Answer? *All three.*

It's simple common sense. You only need two legs to run on a treadmill. That leaves one hand free to point and click and the other hand—and chin—free to fold the laundry. One note of caution: If you come down on the treadmill at the wrong angle, you may fly off it and crash into the wall. As in other aspects of day trading, practice makes perfect.

Stay Motivated

Stress is one underlying cause of burnout, but what are the other reasons that day traders quit this noblest of professions? I don't think they quit because they become physically exhausted, or because they develop serious health problems, or because they have nervous breakdowns and psychotic breaks. Of course, many of them do, but I think that's just a fancy excuse. No, the real reason day traders quit is because they have insufficient motivation—in other words, they *lose the will to trade*.

How does a day trader recover his lost motivation? There are several over-the-counter dietary supplements available today, like Motivex from MojoSource Labs, that have been proven as safe and effective as any other placebo on the market. But what if such remedies do not work for you?

There is one solution that I can confidently recommend to every day trader who is facing down the scourge of burnout: *singing.*

Singing is the secret weapon that has kept me in this crazy game for so long. By starting every morning with an inspirational song, I find myself completely centered—and filled with that sense of well-being that one needs in order to stare at a computer screen for twelve hours and execute hair-trigger trades that could go south at a moment's notice.

What do I sing? Try this inspirational number, sung to the tune of the ballad "I Believe I Can Fly":

I believe I can buy
I believe my stocks will touch the sky
I trade the market every night and day
I'm gonna point-and-click my life away

And, of course, nothing gets the blood pumping more than this number, sung to the tune of "The Theme from *Rocky*":

Duh duh duhhhhhh
Duh duh duhhhhhh
Duh duh duh duh duh
Duh duh duh duh duh duh duh duh duh
Duhhhhhhhhhhhhhhhh

One final note: Make your best efforts to sing these songs when no one else is around. Day traders get a bad enough rap as it is.

CONGRATULATIONS!

You have completed reading the "Ten Principles of Day Trading"— and you are one of the few people ever to make it all the way through to the end.

You are now so steeped in the science of day trading that if you had a conversation with a Wall Street professional, he wouldn't have the slightest idea what you were talking about.

Now it's time to move on to more advanced studies. The final section of this book presents important "Tools of the Day Trader"— valuable information you won't want to do without, even if you find it incomprehensible.

One caveat: Do not attempt to day trade without first reading this important final section. By skipping it, you would be "breaking the chain" of this book and might suffer bad luck as a result. One reader in Oslo, Norway, skipped these final chapters and started day trading anyway, despite the warnings. His computer caught fire, burning his house to a crisp.

Tools

HOT STOCK PICKS

If I had a nickel for every hot stock
somebody told me about,
I'd have thirty-five cents in nickels.

—Chad Halstead, day trader

I'm a big fan of stock-market programs on TV, but there's one thing they do on those shows that really honks me off. They'll have an expert come on and give a series of hot stock picks. Then, just after you've taken the trouble to jot the stock names down on your pizza box, the anchorman will read a wimpy disclaimer to this effect: "The opinions expressed are those of our guest and do not represent recommendations of this program or the network."

Needless to say, you won't be hearing any of that legalistic doubletalk out of this trillionaire. The following stock picks are all surefire investment opportunities for the day trader, and I recommend that you load up on all of them without delay. No disclaimers here—just really great stock picks from a guy who has yet to steer you wrong.

One note: These are all solid companies, not a bunch of fly-by-night flashes-in-the-pan. Therefore, I am recommending them as long-term investments: stocks to buy and hold in your portfolio for five, ten, fifteen minutes or more.

Baboonorgans.com

Medical science long ago anointed baboon organs as a medical miracle—but they have been difficult to come by, usually requiring one to untangle the red tape of doctors, hospitals, organ banks, etc. Not anymore. Baboonorgans.com is the first online marketplace for baboon organs, and all predictions are for explosive growth. "We're not just about baboon hearts," says founder and CEO Jeff Shupansky. "If it's in a baboon, and it can be successfully pulled out of a baboon, we've got it online."

Shupansky promises that initial glitches in the inventory system—which have led to people receiving the wrong organs, no organ at all, or live, angry baboons in a box—are being ironed out.

Market capitalization: $22.4 billion.

Del's Computers

Del's Computers is not to be confused with Dell Computers— although, then again, maybe it is. Founder and CEO Del Huddleston acknowledges that the company's IPO—in which its stock price rocketed from $42 to $376 in a matter of eight minutes—may owe at least some of its success to the fact that people confused it with the more famous computer company. But Huddleston insists that the comparison should stop right there. "For one thing, we don't make computers," he points out. "We make *composters*. That was just a typo." But there's no typo in this high-flying company's bottom line.

Market capitalization: $32.8 billion.

screwtopwines.com

Sometimes going to the corner liquor store for a bottle of your favorite screw-top wine just isn't convenient enough. That was the idea behind screwtopwines.com, the brainchild of Gus "Fuzzy" Ferguson, founder and CEO of this hot new offering. All of your favorite basement-priced hooch is here: Ruby Rocket, Wonderbird, Thrillswill—available online for the first time, and no corkscrew required! "I saw a lot of wines being offered over the Internet," remarks Ferguson, "but they all cost, like, more than four bucks." Ferguson also plans to market a full line of custom-sized brown paper bags that are *de rigeur* for his online customers.

Market capitalization: $40.8 billion.

ePat

There's been an enduring fascination with former First Lady Pat Nixon, and ePat intends to tap into what founder and CEO Willie Kludgian sees as a burgeoning market for Pat Nixon–related products. "It's clear to me that Americans just can't get enough of Pat Nixon—and we're here to make sure that they *do* get enough," he said in a recent conference call with market analysts. Kludgian is offering not just Pat Nixon fashions, cosmetics, and porcelain figurines but also a newly published book, *Pat Under Our Skin: Why We're All Still Crazy About Mrs. Nixon.* Clearly, if the recent three-for-one stock split means anything, investors are wild about Mrs. Nixon, too.

Market capitalization: $42.1 billion.

Things.com

Things.com is the newest and boldest "e-tailer" of things in the marketplace today. Founder and CEO Marilyn Broford is bullish on her company's prospects: "You go on the Internet these days, and you find e-tailers who sell CDs, books, even plane tickets, no problem. But what if you're looking for some things? You have to go here." Having always been interested in things, Broford has turned a lifelong passion into a booming business, and her creation is being cheered from Wall Street to Main Street. Broford plans, in early 2001, to roll out two new spin-offs of the company, specializing in stuff and junk.

Market capitalization: If you have to ask, you can't afford it.

DAY TRADING ACCESSORIES

The most important piece of equipment a day
trader has is his own head, and the second-
most would have to be easy-fit pants.

—Val Modeen, day trader

You'd be surprised how many day traders think that all they need is a computer, a phone line, and a box of Mallomars and they're in business.

Not so.

There are many important day trading accessories on the market today, and for your convenience, they are all for sale on my web site, www.sexytrillionaire.com. Don't feel compelled to buy them—but remember, your competition already *has*.

Here's a selection of some of the top sellers:

Day Trader's Deluxe Software Package

Everything the day trader needs, all on three 100 percent installation-resistant CD-ROM disks. Package includes "Fudgen Financial Wizard," the ideal software for fudging your financial results;

"IgnoreShield for Windows," which immediately deletes distracting "data" that clutter research pages, like profits, earnings, and dividend yield; and "Immolator Deluxe," a video game that has won rave reviews for its ultra-realistic 3-D graphics simulating the evisceration and incineration of pus-spewing alien trolls. *$89.95.*

Day Trader Nutri-Patches

Do you find, like many day traders, that you have no time to eat anymore—but you don't want to mess with IV needles and the like? Problem solved, thanks to Nutri-Patch, by Derm-o-Food Labs. No time to eat those Doritos? Peel off a Nutri-Patch, slap it on your arm, and within seconds, brain-lubricating fat will go rushing to your head. Let's consign old-fashioned "mouth eating" to the scrap heap of obsolete concepts—it's Nutri-Patch to the rescue! Besides Dorito flavor, six-patch strip includes pork rind, pizza, zesty cheese food, and yummy chocolate-chip mint. *$14.95.*

Trade-Z-Boy Inversion Desk

The scientific results are in: Day traders can increase their mental sharpness—and their investment returns—if they day trade while hanging upside down. Once you've been manacled to the comfortable but sturdy Trade-Z-Boy Inversion Desk, the dream of blood rushing to places it doesn't really want to go becomes a reality. Made from two tons of the finest titanium steel; customer must sign form releasing manufacturer from all liability. *$799.95.*

Pocket Shock-It

Are you one of those rare day traders who doesn't let his precarious jerry-built portfolio keep him up at night? Shame on you: While you snore away, the rest of the world is trading—and getting ready to have *you* for breakfast. But thanks to the battery-rechargeable Pocket Shock-It, normal, uninterrupted sleep is a thing of the past. Strap it onto any particularly sensitive part of your anatomy, and this electronic wonder, based on the same state-of-the-art technology that gave us the stun gun, will produce a four-hundred-volt jolt of electricity—enough to get you back in front of your screen in no time flat. Don't let bad overnight movements in your stocks shock you—let this little sucker shock you first! *$49.95.*

Burn-no-Mor Mousepad

We've all been there: We're buying, selling, buying, selling, and buying so fast that our mouse pad bursts into flames, which spread to our pajama sleeve—endangering that all-important next trade. Thanks to the flame-retardant Burn-no-Mor Mousepad, the only thing spontaneously combusting will be your white-hot portfolio! From the innovative geniuses at GeekSolutions, the Burn-no-Mor Mousepad is made of ultra-durable, triple-tested material, guaranteed to stand up to as much as two or three weeks of continuous day trading. Comes in Jennifer Love Hewitt, Tiffany-Amber Thiessen, and Sarah Michelle Gellar. *$17.95.*

Hyper-Hand Robotic Helper

Carpal tunnel syndrome put your mouse-operating hand on the sidelines? There was a time when the idea of a lifelike robot hand wired to the day trader's brain by means of easy-paste electrodes seemed like the stuff of science fiction. But no more: The Hyper-Hand Robotic Helper does everything a human hand can do—except wear out! (Consult your physician. Not recommended for people who are creeped out by the sight of a disembodied hand twitching on their desk all day.) *$189.95.*

The Day Trading Bumper Sticker Collection

In those rare moments when you're away from your screen, let the world know what you do for a living! *Complete set of five: $10.99.*

MY OTHER CAR'S ON eBAY

HONK IF YOU SHORTED COMPAQ

HAVE YOU HUGGED YOUR MOUSE TODAY?

DAY TRADERS DO IT EVERY TWO MINUTES

IF YOU CAN READ THIS, YOUR VISION HAS YET TO BE
RUINED BY STARING AT A COMPUTER SCREEN FOR
FOURTEEN HOURS A DAY WITHOUT A BREAK

FINAL THOUGHTS

Giving
Something Back

I would like to get out in the world and help
others less fortunate than myself, but that
would mean leaving this room.

—Katie Corday, day trader

Early last year, I had a very scary experience—the kind of experience that every day trader, regardless of his bravado, secretly dreads.

While taking a shower in the morning, I suddenly felt a strange
sensation. At first, I thought that this strange sensation might just
have been what it feels like to take a shower, since I hadn't had one
in some time. But then the signs became unmistakable—a tingling
and numbness in my right hand and wrist, gradually working its
way up my right arm.

That's right. I was feeling the symptoms associated with carpal
tunnel syndrome, a terrible affliction that has cut short the careers of
day traders even more dedicated and talented than I.

I went to the doctor immediately, and that's when I got the good
news: It wasn't CTS after all, but merely an incurable circulatory ail-
ment. I felt as though I had dodged a bullet, but this "close call" was

also a "wake-up call." I had to face the facts: I wasn't going to be able to day trade forever.

I made a decision, then and there. I would cut back my trading hours from eighteen to sixteen, and I would devote those extra two hours to philanthropy—"giving something back."

As day traders, we are blessed. Not only are we our own bosses, we're also our own secretaries, our own receptionists, and our own plant-watering ladies. On that fateful day in the doctor's office, right after I pocketed some aspirin samples, I recognized the importance of sharing this blessing with others. My mission, simply put, was this: to try to turn everyone in the world into a day trader.

It's not an easy task. There are underdeveloped regions of, say, New Guinea, where entire villages exist without a modem. I will not rest until everyone living in those villages, from chieftain to shaman, has a heavily leveraged margin account.

A little closer to home, I've spoken at schools, teaching children as young as four or five about the principles of day trading by telling them a little fable I call "Jack and the eStock." In it, a little boy named Jack trades options in two stocks, eCow and magic-beans.com, and becomes a trillionaire. People thought that kinder-gartners were too young to grasp the science of day trading, but I'm proud to say that many of my little students are now trading online, using Mommy and Daddy's retirement funds without their knowl-edge.

How can you, as a day trader, "give something back"? You may not have the free time that I do. You may not be a master communi-cator like me, capable of convincing millions of people to do your bidding with a mere nod or a wink. Regardless, there is still some-thing you can do for the cause of day trading:

Buy more copies of this book and give one to every person you know.

It doesn't seem like much, but try it and see. You'll be surprised what a warm feeling this simple act of charity will give you.

A Fond Farewell

Our journey is now at an end. I hope that you've found our journey together educational and stimulating, although not in a sexual way.

Speaking for myself, the mere act of writing this book has been a learning process, as I discovered just how much I *didn't* know about certain topics—and had to make up information to fill in the gaps. Thank you for the opportunity to learn side by side with you.

As you start to day trade, like a young sparrow taking flight from its nest, I look upon you with a mixture of optimism and pride and hope that you don't crash beak first into the many plateglass windows that await you.

Should we ever meet face to face, chances are you'll be a trillionaire by then. At that point, I'll teach you the trillionaire's secret handshake and give you directions to the ultra-exclusive private club in Singapore where only trillionaires are allowed to shake their groove-things—and where the napkins are made out of money.

Until then, let me leave you with these final words of wisdom:

- Any stock worth buying is worth selling four minutes later.

- The best trades you make will be the ones you do by mistake.

- What your trades lack in quality they'll make up for in quantity.

- Don't get bogged down by "numbers."

- Buy now, ask questions later.

- If it sounds too good to be true—*go for it.*

And now, if you don't mind, I have to go check my stocks.